Oriental Floral Designs and Motifs

for Artists, Needleworkers and Craftspeople

MING-JU SUN

Dover Publications, Inc.
New York

Publisher's Note

This book provides artists, needleworkers and craftspeople with floral illustrations usable in a variety of ways. The full-page unified designs are complete patterns in themselves; the smaller motifs are individual spots that can be used directly or repeated and combined to create larger patterns; and there are also border elements. These designs and motifs encompass not only the strictly floral—a variety of representative Oriental flowers such as peony, wistaria and lotus; cherry and plum trees in full bloom; and many kinds of herbaceous plants including bamboo—but also the associated animal life, such as grasshoppers climbing plant stalks, and birds, bees and butterflies active amid the blossoms. All of these natural forms are rendered with the combination of elegance and precision characteristic of Far Eastern art.

Copyright © 1985 by Amie Sun Ambrose (Ming-ju Sun).
All rights reserved under Pan American and International Copyright Conventions.

Published in Canada by General Publishing Company, Ltd., 30 Lesmill Road, Don Mills, Toronto, Ontario.
Published in the United Kingdom by Constable and Company, Ltd., 10 Orange Street, London WC2H 7EG.

Oriental Floral Designs and Motifs for Artists, Needleworkers and Craftspeople is a new work, first published by Dover Publications, Inc., in 1985.

DOVER *Pictorial Archive* SERIES

This book belongs to the Dover Pictorial Archive Series. You may use the designs and illustrations for graphics and crafts applications, free and without special permission, provided that you include no more than ten in the same publication or project. (For permission for additional use, please write to Dover Publications, Inc., 31 East 2nd Street, Mineola, N.Y. 11501.)

However, republication or reproduction of any illustration by any other graphic service whether it be in a book or in any other design resource is strictly prohibited.

Manufactured in the United States of America
Dover Publications, Inc., 31 East 2nd Street, Mineola, N.Y. 11501

Library of Congress Cataloging in Publication Data

Sun, Ming-ju.
  Oriental floral designs and motifs for artists, needleworkers, and craftspeople.

  (Dover pictorial archive series)
  1. Decoration and ornament—Plant forms—East Asia. 2. Decoration and ornament—East Asia—Themes, motives. I. Title. II. Series.
NK1482.S86 1985   745.4   85-4548
ISBN 0-486-24903-4

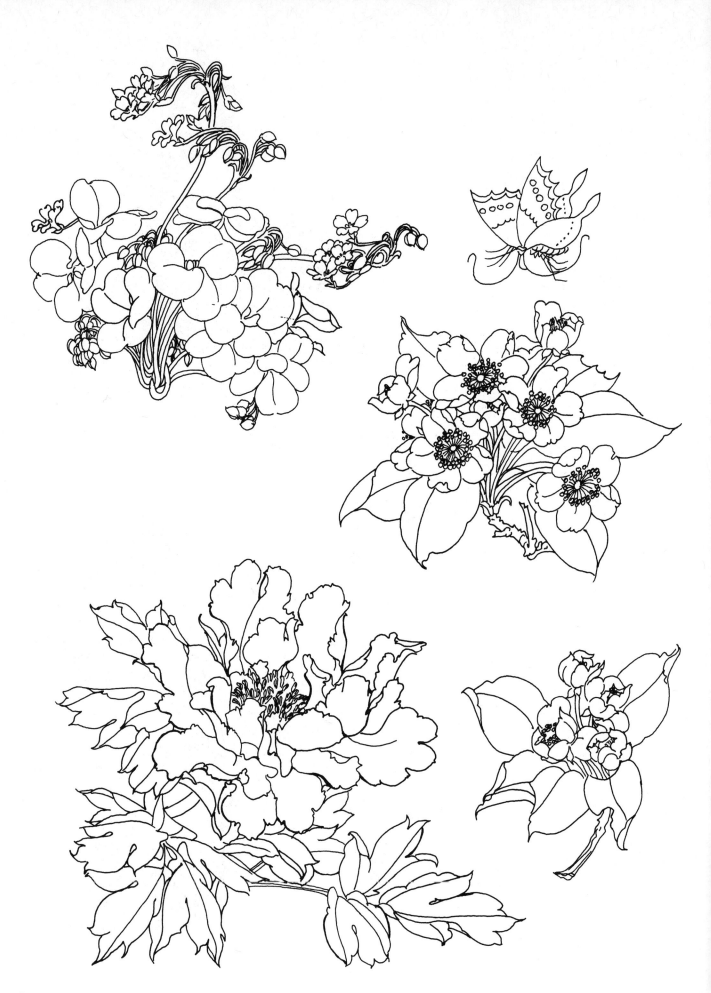

9

16

17

19

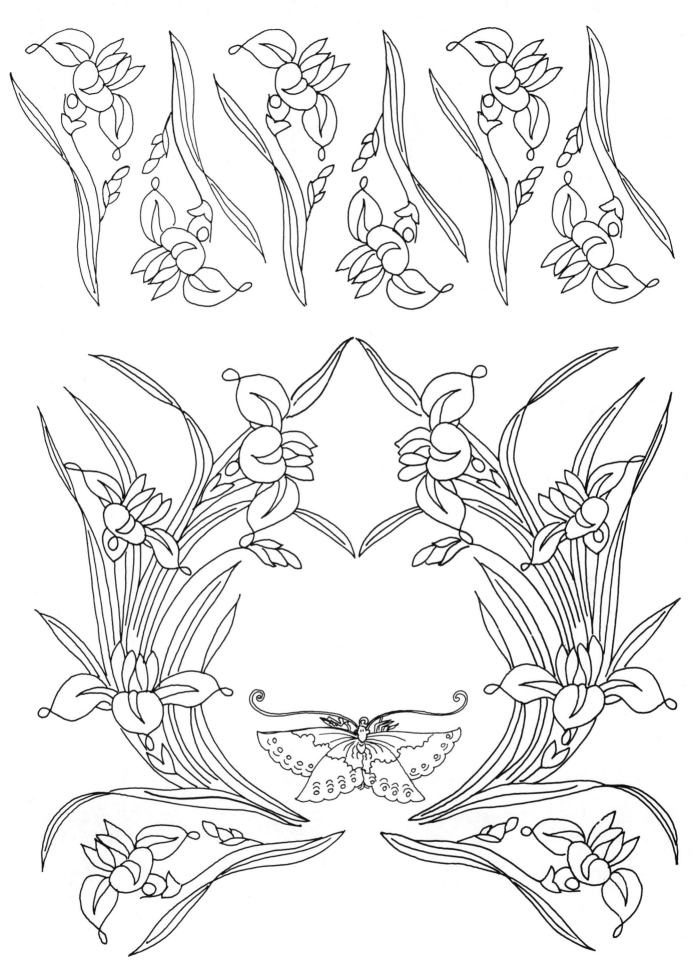

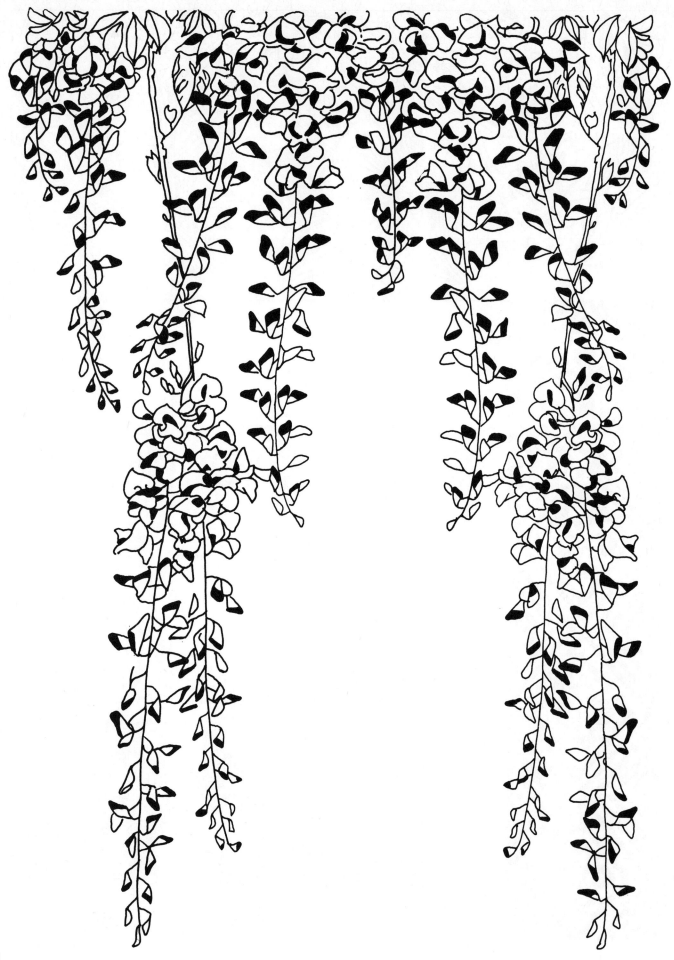

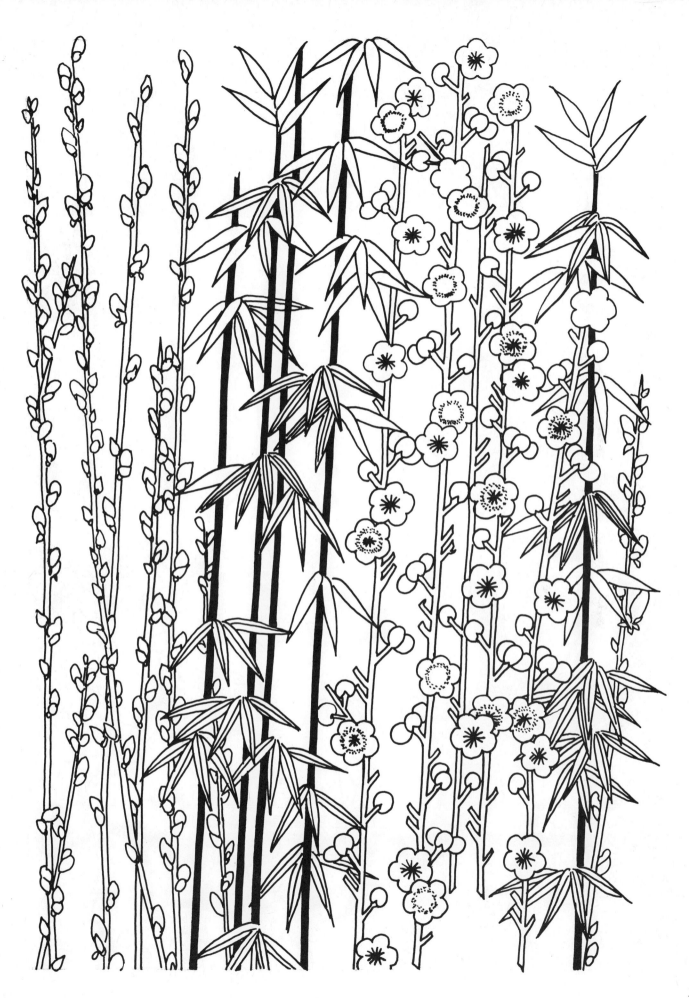

31

35

44

61

70

83